Zombie Jet

Zombie Jet

Connie Deanovich

Zoland Books
Cambridge, Massachusetts

First edition published in 1999 by
Zoland Books, Inc.
384 Huron Avenue
Cambridge, Massacusetts 02138

FIRST EDITION

Book design by Janis Owens
PRINTED IN THE UNITED STATES OF AMERICA

06 05 04 03 02 01 00 99   8 7 6 5 4 3 2 1

This book is printed on acid-free paper, and its binding materials have been
chosen for strength and durability.

.

Library of Congress Cataloging-in-Publication Data
Deanovich, Connie, 1960-
    Zombie Jet / Connie Deanovich.
        p.   cm.
    ISBN 1-58195-010-1
    I. Title.
PS3554.E1744Z454   1999   99-29915
811'.54–dc21   CIP

*"Home! How lucky to
have one, how arduous
to make this scene
of beauty for
your family and
friends."*

James Schuyler

Acknowledgments

These poems were originally published in the following magazines and anthologies.

"American Avalon" and "Frankenstein" in *Bomb* edited by Jenifer Berman, "Frankenstein" also anthologized in *Real Things: An Anthology of Popular Culture in American Poetry* edited by Jim Elledge and Susan Swarthout.

"In India" in *The World* 53 edited by Ed Friedman and Jo Ann Wasserman.

"This is the Universe," "You Don't have to be Slick," "The Three Times," "Porno Stars With Tuberculosis" in *Gas 8* and "King Kong Watches Over Me" in *Gas 9* edited by Kevin Opstedal.

"Sestina Salutations to Rodrigo Toscano" in *Tinfish*.

"Dedicated to the Advancement of Learning" in *Mike and Dale's Younger Poets summer 1997* edited by Michael Price and Dale Smith.

"Accessories" and "Confessional Piano" in *Bathos Journal 1* edited by Dan Mosher.

"Leonardo Da Vinci Ocean" and "Breakfast Sea" in *American Letters & Commentary 7* edited by Anna Rabinowitz and Jeanne Beaumont.

"Little Lake Egypt," "Satan," and "Cyclops Has One Gesture" in *Spoon River Quarterly vol. 22 no. 1* guest edited by Jim Elledge.

"Requirements for an Addiction to Movies" in *Grand Street 62* poetry edited by William Corbett.

"Cult of Clarity" and "Hedonism" in *Graffiti Rag 3* edited by Hayan Charara and Erik Fahrenkopf.

"Marie Antoinette Ocean" in *Parnassus 19.2* collected by August Kleinzahler for editor Herb Leibowitz, and also published in *New American Writing* edited by Paul Hoover and Maxine Chernoff.

"Formerly Communist Love Sonnet" in *Greensboro Review winter 1998-1999* edited by Martin Arnold.

"Permission Gardens" in *American Letter & Commentary* edited by Jeanne Beaumont and Anna Rabinowitz.

"Así Es Colombia" in *Luna* edited by Ray Gonzalez.

Thanks is given to these editors as well as to the Mrs. Giles Whiting Foundation for a Whiting Writers Award and to the anonymous person who nominated me for this award. Special thanks to Bill Corbett and Jane Timken.

Also, "Onward!" to David.

Contents

King Kong Watches Over Me

This is the Universe

The Three Times

1
The Future

tomorrow is a statue

alone like a pink car

the gondolier turns in Italy

simple as a brook

control migrates and dips

sobs into a handkerchief

so happy to be free

you a ship's light

your eyes accumulating

I could smoke your glance

but am engaged to this cello

bossed by illusion

sometimes the top comes off

forming another vintage

skirts that kissed the ground

power in the palm of a hand

order is only an element

ocean liners with clear electroplated details

are still the chance you take

you're almost back

brain red as a tuning fork

wishing for rain

like a hand that extends from the balcony

2
The Present

The birds come for popcorn

because of the words that match them

the sky is sky

but here the sky includes an odor

the soft white blouse I am wearing

I am wearing and anticipating

the twitching throat of an iridescent songbird

the songbird and the skyline

the skyline and the ground

how big can these buildings possibly be?

and feel a connection to Malaysia because of this?

I have nothing to do with basketball

but a cake shaped as one is being cooked partly for me

the heart has certain capacities

a dull statue of a brown horse takes a lot of loving

In America

the middle of it

great big lake slapping up beside

3
The Past

let's say it's wonderful

gold on golden embroidery

heavy with ducks

an aquatic thematic shadow

big tease for those who never

see water

yesterday a cinematic curtain

Humphrey Bogart

complex as a shoe shine

Judy Garland

simple as sin

a splash of soda to connect it

a farm mind

sex thrust deep into the mending

walking like a widow

across the baseball field

wind the size of

back there

beside personal crescendo

the shots rang out and were soothing

the ghost of Mrs. Muir's sat in a chair

you hold a hand like this

wait for several more dinners to pass

for certain bells to ring

American Avalon

Knock the zoo out of your eye, the sand dollar with dried babies or
dried money inside. All along this beach the view is the same. It's
you waving from a pastel balcony, and everyone knows you're the
kind of woman who can cook family chicken. A sparkling pan of vi-
sion with an abundance of front and sides is an array reserved for
the moneyed, so here's a 1920s man on a postcard. They always
wore suits then even when the vision is of him waving from a cart of
grapes. In the American Avalon this is the cart of conveyance and he
is the dead I carry to the paradise of my collections.

When the vision is of a society matron decked out for an Arabian
Nights charity function the ghosts that stomped her grapes into wine
dwell here. We don't want to waste cake so the stripper pops out of
a hat instead. At the party to celebrate free speech and humor
through flippancy you say Listen, didn't mean to come off as a
preachy pornographer, and then we hug, our arms encircling like
balletic islanders. Why celebrate notions anyway, or achievements?
Why collapse onto the grass reading a book about the Kickapoo
Indians who lived in this very section of Illinois? Perhaps exactly
where the mailbox is they too set out tokens to friends. That the to-
kens may've been dried squirrel kidneys is excessively factual, and
how can this addition to knowledge substitute for a party anyway?
The fact that Brezhnev's widow admits she fell for him because of his
eyebrows is a better substitute, but won't there be a Day of the Dead
party or some kind of party some time in the future? Our myths are
about to stagnate like James Baldwin, and our visions are contained
in a drawer.

What you need is an infantry of desires to ransack your life, to get
you bloody before the grape cart comes to trundle you off to the

beach you'll never leave. Even in a dump there is the mirage that saves you, the glass in the ugly houses that can redden, the fresh new interesting piano and flute music that can come out of some of them. Then a voice suggesting a reputation built around a canopied bed doles out the last shred of its Southern strength and you hear it but then it's gone. Wanting is chronic. The ratio of longing to actual splash in the pool. It's a conspiracy the idea of beauty. The condition of the sky is distributed unequally, but at least it's sky you can breathe. If this old notion of beauty stopped being invisible and rotated around you like a stranger doing the fire dance would you collapse? Maybe one packet of splendor per day set onto your lap like a puppy.

Expectations of the Environment

That it be beautiful
that the candy be from a factory not poisonous
that the hair nets worn there be fresh as freshman
that the room have
if not a dramatic wallpaper
at least the feeling that it does.
If there is a clock
that it be either the ticking or silent kind
no humming
no humming like the senile
no cats no eczema.
But breath somehow instead
in the wide arrangement of whatever furniture
or no furniture if the only choice is a corduroy couch.
That there be pockets for possibilities
an alto recorder laying out or beginner's vibrator
or veteran's baseball bat.
There is nothing oceanic about it.
Wobble about on the earth for a while sailors
that the space holding you be made by you
absolute affectation
Kennedy profile paperweight on the electric bill.
What guides your guiding spirit except to see things
red as the tip of a tiny smoking monkey
from the gum machine.
That until a Korean girl is born
grows up mean and moves to DeKalb
takes pottery and makes a salad bowl of great beauty
use only its shadow
the greater the radish the lettuce the onion
the better your life.
That which calls you forth is what
like an architect his cupola
you set up in advance of agony
in anticipation of expectation
the wooden whatever you know intimately and go towards
the tin and wool and Madras cloth

the fox fur collar the black leather case a baritone is in
baby yellow tulips four or five to a pot
the pine dresser stabbed who knows when by who knows who
whose drawer pulls are polished and battered, saved from the
garbage. And when the sun comes in how does it come through what
glass of what age and quality
and what does it warm and what is beneath?

In India

The sun is such a jerk, shoving heat like snowballs down everyone's neck. But it's not a game. It's a death toll of 436. Only death is sped up in Uttar Pradesh where the power of slowness spreads out like oversized buttocks across the state. The flag of the soaked hanky is raised but does not waft in the absent wind. Summer's heat wave is in attendance, raising temperatures like alarmed hands at baby prison roll call. The flirtatious populace of Bombay arrives black against the sunshine to greet you. They bring a cow. They bring tea in little glass cups.

The cloth of your history wilts then is stolen. You have become another person—a white person with a banished stomach. Write in your notebook a thousand times "there is no such thing as culture shock."

A bath is a prayer, so little American boys must be sinners here. A ship with two young American honeymooners sails the Indian Ocean. They wave at you from Absent-Minded Class, and you, having read this, return the gesture. In the villages gestural meanings are just as clear. You are poor there, your hand held out as if a skinny bird should land.

In the Himalayas and elsewhere, the past causes vertigo—Gandhi and Nehru's historic acts seen through dizzy eyes. The insinuating tones of *British Rule*. Other ideas, such as the religion of beauty, were never born—not organically with blood—and so have no place in the caste system. But the idea of the untouchables (who were very born with lots of blood), has lost its place due to the legal system. What is the best system for eating a vegetarian meal? In exactly what order do the yogurts go and the insane pickles? Food has the personality you have, so watch who you are, and, if Buddhist or Hindu, who you were.

Shall We Gather at the River?

You are your own gathering
with soft secluded fireflies resting on medium
around your collar

A gathering is an adequate symbol of itself
a gathering of everyone you've ever known
now frozen in individual serving size times
in the brain like bees trapped in different versions
of the Coke bottle

The money of the people of your life
their hearts from rich to diluted
and moonshine hearts are favorites
vast and homemade and fun loving
willing to share like songbirds

These hearts you'd thaw out and use again
put lipstick on them
give them glasses
sit within them
as if moonshine hearts were a riverbank

Uganda Unpeopled

Bwindi-Impenetrable Forest, Uganda. The Bwindi-Impenetrable Forest. The Impenetrable Forest. The gorillas are moving back to the impenetrable forest. It is time reversed. The impenetrable forest time of mountain gorillas is a romantic haven protected by the fiery stakes I plant around the words *Bwindi-Impenetrable Forest*. Nature also follows trends only in a much grander way complete with creation. This what you are reading is a park, and at the gate you are reminded to concentrate on the image of a newly-blossoming purple iris, such as the plant I have before me. Then to this I've added an animal that isn't there—to the purple iris an orange tiger.

But you can add your own complimentary color, perhaps a brown slash of crop-raiding baboons. And at this gate you are to stop forever because the forest is impenetrable, and impenetrable is a human word meant for human beings like you. You may, however, offer your report—how you have observed villagers tending their beehives, protecting themselves with goodwill. The goodwill of the impenetrable forest is this fist shaken in your face. KEEP OUT, BUSTER! The gorillas expect to sleep their way into the future without you watching as if a now-unemployed agent of Idi Amin.

When it rains in the Bwindi-Impenetrable Forest, perhaps the next time you're in the shower soaping yourself up slick as a snake, one gorilla will scratch his ear and yawn. But you can add your own gestures and activities if you wish, perhaps a nitrogen-fixing tree soaked to the bark swaying in the wet wind with movements as regular as a great vegetarian jaw.

Samoan Sestina

It's daybreak, time to start sitting.
The pillows are piled inside the fales,
and morning begins in Western Samoa.
People here are large and live mostly in villages
where life is scented, robust, and slow.
"Talofa," they say. "Talofa!"

Welcome, hello, and goodbye all mean talofa,
which you can practice saying, sitting
with a palm leaf in your hands, slowly
letting yourself adjust to life in a fale,
a house with no walls in a village
named Vatia, Amerika Samoa.

There are two Samoas,
but both use talofa
as a greeting in villages.
In the South Pacific they sit
side by side like neighboring fales,
but one is "progressing" more slowly.

Western Samoa's approach to change is slow,
but it's faster and uglier in America Samoa.
In Pago Pago the Rainmaker Hotel echoes a fale,
but the heart's gone from its talofa.
Near the tuna canneries pinch your nose and sit
watching rainbow buses shuttle workers to villages.

The men play cricket in villages
and endure elaborate tattooing, and slow
paths to wealth that never comes. Sitting
is a popular stance in both Samoas,
smoke from the cooking fires signalling talofa,
the 6 pm curfew bells filling the fales.

Most Christians here pray in a church fale,
one white and floral church per village.

At 6 pm outsiders do *not* receive a warm *talofa*
and must leave or go slow
when caught at dusk in rural Samoa,
which, at curfew, stops moving, prays, and sits.

It's best to sit cross-legged in a family's fale
while visiting a Samoan village
with slow Polynesian beauty and *talofa*.

Key Largo

Illinois

Florida

as if the sounds were queer flowers
as if stretching an overdressed line between the two
as if at the buzzer an Illinoisan watches *Key Largo*

>   Humphrey Bogart (battling again in a boat)

>   "the evil at home"

>   the black and white smoking

>   wet fog tactile and sweaty as movie sin

A woman or man
like a plant tattooed *private* and *green*
puts down roots to be good

>   Learn love's transferability from this

>   and that one thing's for certain (Nature's the boss

>   like when a body slumps into a corner of ocean

>   like when an ocean passes out on a wooden hotel)

A wooden hotel can preside
if you're drawn to think in buildings

>   A room for every mood

And if particularly drawn

Each completely furnished

Formerly Communist Love Sonnet

The Chinese concubine feeling has left and the
sky hovers like the preparation of a revolutionary speech.
You, my long walk with all that expectation
the sexy lunches, thousands of them,
and then all that religion of eroticism.
Beneath the squeeze on my heart is a stranglehold.
You, like a little Italian porcelain village that's all over the
shop window saying *admire this image of foreverness.*

The red scarf is factory-made but silky
and it's what I'd flutter over your face if you were here
and it would be cheap greasy hypnotism, my own malarkey
and we'd be on the southside, at the boat docks, and
I'd kiss you beside the stretch of a Russian grain ship, its
hammer and sickle like the sending out of rescue choppers.

Italian Imagination

Because luminous. Come sit down at this table, wooden as a stage.
Take *my* place and this embroidered pillow. Listen. The jeweled
opera singer tells the tall air regrets instead of observing the over-
sized omens. Observe them: a moon with an organic throat, Buddha
standing wearing pearls. Then vanish like the footprints of this fact:
each year in Italy 12 million people experience devil trouble then
consult the Yellow Pages. The magus arrives in a taxi with a leopard-
skin interior. She knocks at the door using a tiny unmade bed. Her
black trash bag is cool to the trust. Singing is involved here too, as
well as a special slow way to carry a box. Would you care for some
completion? Perhaps a splash of crescendo? Ancient ruins sit in traf-
fic but were themselves once modern unpolluted fascinations, stag-
nant ones. How marvelous Italy looks on a map, perceptible even to
the geographically leaden and satellites.

Formerly fascist. A fistful of death. Florence. Flowers of the
Renaissance garden distilled as the site of costume porn. She drops
her bouquet; he picks it up then he does then she does. A porn star
parliamentarian fighting a custody battle. Land of battles and unim-
peachable boots. The syrup sipped until the rocky world caught up
to Galileo. Guiseppe Verdi means Joe Green. I bring him home for
french fries, beer, and barbecued ribs. Tell him this is how my family
celebrates—condensed.

Gina Lollobrigida. Obscured by vegetation. My customers are birds
who eat popcorn in the theater of my garden then fly to other
venues. *Buon giorno,* birds. Then, *ciao!* The birds defined by cathe-
drals are also welcome, but I have no bells with which to lure them.
I don't know the lures of heaven. Endlessness makes me nervous. I

try to recall the best Catholic plan. An urge to visit Rome as barometer for the devout? Maybe you think otherwise. Such as: science in a farmer's field sneaks up on everyone then changes the entire world. As in a headline. But look at it through this lovely panel of lace. Have some wine and olives. Physical principles are involved here in the spiritual. Take your shoes off and walk toward what is most essential.

Germany Gigantic

Surroundings of a long-suffering wife forced to hang pictures of Bavarian kings. Next door her neighbor arrested in his pajamas. He called the fierce storm holy, began unburying knives. A stein or else travel the world like Robert Louis Stevenson looking for health. He ended up in Samoa. Some Nazis went to South America. Is South America really the ends of the earth? Imagine the time of the Flugelhorn village not the global village.

Alpine + compound = Hitler. What I agree with is an aesthetic judgment along with all the other judgments. Hitler also ruined the beauty of a mountain. Dark legends go with cold air. In Hamburg the Beatles were not the positive flip side of The Rolling Stones. Today the young sing athletic songs. Travel there?

Opera shrunk into an elaborate necklace for a man with a hairy chest. The story is love illicit, delivered daily with heaping grunts of silence. The long silent murder by asphyxiation in *Torn Curtain*. In the countryside silence announces the world's last call. There is no point to getting up early just to hear a huge amount of silence if you don't want to. There's no balance in that. The full power of the sun comes through a pinhole. That's power enough.

This is the Universe

to show it's special
the universe is silver
like a necklace in a diner

to show it's expansive
the universe is a ghost ship
covered up by a leaking cloud

clump together
the animal kingdom
and all of the moons

when it's the universe
what part remains separate?
time because of its voodoo?

time is vodka in a shot glass
that stays the same
even when it's on fire

space is very pleasing
like syncopation
widening at the center

bloodhounds circling are prophets
of the world's worst news but then
stretch out dusty and dumb on the porch

sleeping they stretch like the universe
while more suns than you can imagine
come into being and end

Earth's England

Pink map burning. Across the mantelpiece many emblems of choice—how to parade, when to parade, who to parade for. A dog dozing by the fire is the best career. Either be him or provide for him. Sitting inside/beside the ideal idea. Though even the best city's been bombed, an order as melodious as the flunking vocabulary of a vibrating drunk. The orderliness of tea caught up in a kidnap bag.

In the name of John Paul George & Ringo. In the name of the noise of the British past, as if noise could return like lips to this cup and shimmer like a coatcheck girl, first day on the job, beautiful and safe in the cloakroom. The cloak of Sherlock Holmes was made of fog and tobacco smoke and was a great, oozing, Romantic brain symbolized by a textile to make it British.

The appearance of an idiot begins the comedy. The window is thrown open. Two palace guards, with big, fierce, bushy hats and neck straps look out into the camera then smile soft as skywriting in reverse. In London Zoo the best ape's name is Sir Herbert, and he holds court by sleeping among the apple peels. His keeper arrives dressed as Shakespeare for the benefit of school kids.

And now, in the dark but elsewhere, we can concentrate on the words *melting tomb of the frozen wood frog*. But the fairies still won't arrive, and magic, like beginning and end, is lost in the eternities of past and future. Magic still sleeps in its bed, offering only a rolling countryside laboring to give some impression of movement to those who want large-scale amazement. And then, of every metal and compound, bells ring. One from every century, and that's just for starters.

Macedonian Movie

Pilgrimage to a dialect. The character of the photographer often mentions his cock, strangely, not his eye. In *Before the Rain* all eyes look up at the clouds, but violence grows down below the belt. Sometimes it rises to a dozen slugs to the gut. Sometimes it breaks a heart. This is as high as it gets. In the London restaurant the busboy is beaten by a fellow Bosnian. He shows him where his dick is, as if this gesture is a weapon. The other returns with a gun, even though the Brits have politely resumed eating their meals, giving ethnic cleansing violence a palate cleansing break. When the photographer wins his Pulitzer and loses patience with his London lover, he resumes the life he left in Macedonia sixteen years ago, but he resumes wrong.

Donkeys as part of the family. Alex is part of the village covering a hillside near the sea, the village that shoots him. It is a scene of well-worn beauty. You bite your nails bloody because of it. You dip your ragged fingers in a bowl of *bucolic,* but they still sting. Land of rock worn smooth and the automatic weapon. Yet the world is innocent and beautiful. Automation takes thinking out of the process. Puts speed there instead. Here, in the village, everything is slow to change. Have a smoke, a shot of grain alcohol.

Monastery scene of love. To pray for the dead is the most exciting prayer. The young monk is thrown from devotions by a sexy foot. He must leave his cell for his grave. Bullet to the head, but pray for him first. Where is refuge? Behind the lace curtains in the shot-out house where once it was peaceful? In the Muslim house where the women are waiters? In the church where the priests practice harmony? In the birth of a new bloody sheep then brandy and talk of fucking sexy women? In the dead bloated body of the sex-mad shepherd? Should we wail like his mother at his deathbed or keep our hungers to ourselves? Make our hungers into trefoil symbols and hang them on our ancient walls? Hungers start with physical activation and include the flickerings of art. Art stands for better times. Times here are bad. Smoke a cigarette. "It's an asylum."

Strawberries, Optimistic Version

one day in a restaurant
by an adequate candle
peace will come like a hand across the table
and it will say things
and the vest you wear
will be like sunshine
only controlled
and even though the day collapses
into a dark like plastic
you will sleep
and it will be OK
all will be in step
like the All-American Rockettes
who've made it because of their genetic factors
and who one day upon retirement
may visit less criminal places
personal ambassadors with a remembrance of outrageous hats that
once signified some concept
something like strawberries that have taken sunshine
and soil and combined them into the end of an encounter
that stands for something

Silver Dress and Ukulele

Out of Chicago

We should feel a good storm
a Midwestern storm
going blind with power
while we watch laughing
eating cheap beige cookies
on a rock solid porch

My pet, my toy
bring wind that comes right in
and rain so sloppy it's arrested for vagrancy

And when the moon or sun glows
like a big disc of red plastic vinyl
and bats sparkle like patent leather
let's remember it's a place like
Lucky's Toy Store and Towers
that names our inner rivers

Así Es Colombia

The motif is the man's shoes with fat, checkerboard heels. The motif is fifty cars, cleaned and detailed for Saturday night parked on a side street whose history is scattered.

The motif has tentative furniture in case it won't last and cooks recipes strangers suggest at the meat counter. The motif is no perfection beyond a walk down Byron Street, no walk salted down and naked by Ballanchine, no walk carved out of *Taxi Driver*, no Biblical walk through a prop desert, or military march into ambush or annals.

The motif stretches out its hand to you all kissy-face, except it's for real, and all the places never set foot in are set in now, all that talk lit up like a hungry/horny date now, and who knew this is how the language would land—still raw as a horny virgin dipped in the image of a slut.

What was known by the motif was known by the laundress, famous for having been in prison and for smoking all over the folded clothes. Laverne. Laverne the shakes and smokes define you. The bad home permanent defines you. Your mother defines you/afraid of you. The motif had dangerous friends from coffee shops and thrift store aisles who disguised themselves as poor women. The motif knew the widow of the inventor of sugar, and she was poor now so buy her a piece of blueberry pie.

The motif wants comfort from you, big sweetie. Tell it that truth stands for version. Where can you turn to find the direction of the nearest clock factory now? Where is the needle factory, and why is this loss so important? Who invented the zipper, Chicago style, the snap, Chicago style, the famous key ring with a choice is stuff that used to be pointable. There. From there. And at night, the motif heard the quiet that a factory without a serial killer could give.

The motif was sitting by the plant's window as they came to the nightclub in out-of-fashion Cuban heels (why?). The sign and signified of another elite.

The motif stretches its hand to you for more future, so it, like the flag of the United States of America, can go on with its praise and punishments, the bookends of life. The motif should really be riding between *serve* and *protect* on a Chicago squad car, hanging onto its side like air from Saturday nights, both perfect air and imperfect air, the air to gamble in, or the air with which to wait.

The motif could be so frightened it would have to blank out, believing that Picasso or Cézanne or Madam Curie or The Beatles or the big successful strip club near the house would open its world/doors of intelligence/ruination to it. The motif wants much more of the world so defines even its footprints with something balanced between sacramental cloth and whacked-out scratchy leopard skin. The motif defines you too by what words are forming as you push these away, and down the street isn't down the street anymore but all this enclosure that sets itself up to be the Hot Shot of the neighborhood, the slicked-up adventurer with a theme-from-Mexico car horn, otherwise recognizable by a colorful nature and elusiveness that can't speak for itself.

Silver Dress and Ukulele

These can always
be trusted

Though they're
not the symbols
of home
they are the symbols of home

The world
comes from
the stores
that are closest
to the heart
the stores
that cannot stay
or that stay
forever

And if we
don't live off
the land

And if we
crave what
is crass
and lowly

And find
comfort in
such a hot dog stand
finding citizenship
where everyone
throws their
wrappers away

Then there we are

Reading a book
on a platform

Wearing clothes
that look odd in the woods

Tomorrow we'll
collapse into
a breakfast
booth and
write out
checks there
having made life work
another month

And here is
where we
find respite
drinking coffee

The world a window

Dedicated to the Advancement of Learning

like hunger in a bird
      the moment shows up as a rash of nervousness
            a neck straining after disappearing speech

up the stairs of the library
      passing the momentary daffodils
            is such a wonderful feeling

getting out of a bath when it's warm out
      laying down next to a pizza
            birds singing outside but really it's bats

up the stairs of the library
      is really so much more honest
            than ascending the stairs

if it's dishonesty that's called for
      then at least let it be fabulous
            a Roman chiffon drape on a balcony

across the New Orleans Cemetery
      with its graves above ground
            wafts heat as hot as conquered Egypt

it would be nice not to think of things
      in terms of hot or cold, putting thoughts
            into temperatures like a night nurse

but you try living
      in the middle of a continent
            and not notice temperature

even at the Chagall Windows
      in the clammy Art Institute
            where you're supposed to be warm you're cold

up the stairs of the library
    we ascend toward all that language
        and it challenges us like a wobbly boat

Ted Berrigan said
    "goodbye house"
        "its ironing board, by moonlight"

and in a house challenged by eau de strawberry jam
    piano lessons are taught by a grown-up geek which
        was a training ground for noticing the essentials

Small but Big

be everything
all day
and all night
like a giant bell
be time
and music
be up in the sky and expensive
and down to earth and expensive
look like you look
which is
absolutely gorgeous
my arms around you
like the sea
my toes
sliding alongside your leg
like a sleek train of the future
come on with that mouth
tasty as perfect pitch
heartbeat chinking away
like a bank of tollbooths

be the vice
and the warning
and the cure
lift my spirits
with your pinky
your eyes
like a refreshment stand
selling Coca-Cola
with chips of ice
my intemperate nature
in the cool shade of your cabana
open 24 hours a day
every day
specials each noon

red and white stripes

You Don't Have to be Slick

Salted bird out of a coarse cloth bag
will do for dinner out in the gloss of the glossy garden.
Your mouth maneuvers the bones like a majorette. Would definitely
not want you maneuvering into the clothy containments of a wood-
happy restaurant wearing Italian loafers with a tasseled beak.

These three rosewood beads are what you *really* own of Blackbird
Mansion. Would *positively* hate seeing you smile at the maitre d' the
same way you smile at the rosy babies of our acquaintance. The
tweed look is no way the look for you. Rather you held a flashlight
on a frog.

Take this gray pinstriped rock and smack it against a boulder. Stand
in the dust drinking from a plaid canteen, the remaining birds float-
ing away toward high-profile careers in navigation and propagation.

Movies for the Sister Kathy

For you I climbed *The Exorcist* staircase
To you from Hollywood's summer
I toss the opening grenade

Sweat with me in a broken theater
With horror movies to sell
Grow fur on your hands with me

Whistle "Nazis Coming" with me
Play invisible maracas with me
Sway and spin

Let's throw rock salt on each other's brains
Bliss of a huge garlic pickle
Bliss of the artificial sky of Arabian heaven

I want you in a movie I want you in a silver gown
And silver wig that quivers want you to unhinge
Under the strain of extraterrestrial power

Call you Xylene give you a kingdom
Announce your marriage to a colony of ants
Feed you smooth slabs of synthetics

We want to sit in the movies and
Snarl and snap and sugar
We want to roll our bald heads down the aisle

Like from a guillotine
To gutlessly endure
To kick each other the codes

We want a shiny car for two
Like for dolls
We want to go from movie to movie

Accumulating gestures
Let's freeze beneath the largest screen
Images inducing in us both another identical temperament

Oh for a small friendly android
Who doesn't bat the eyes she doesn't have
No matter how many times we order The Persuasion

Like a bridge I suspend belief over Lake Artifice
Manufacture curiosity with me
An eyebrow raised by the close-up of the clock

Our eyes are happiest when busy
Winking like a mysterious desert
Cinematically this is our most inconclusive

Yet reliable signal
Violins are there crescendoing
Then they crescendo for us as well

Wishes for Dan

tacos crispy
and sparkling
and a blue train
shiny
as an apple
also a wide
brown field
big and interesting enough
(for your kindness)
to walk in
and an oddball hat
designed only for
serving little sandwiches
at an immense prom
and a boxy suitcase
with a brown silk lining
clicking open
as if it were
the solution

good idea too
to remember
to add flowers
which help
when thinking backwards
through time
and also
I press into your hand
a token
that makes you tremble
but you choose how
I send choice to you
because who's a dictator?
and lethargy too
lay around Dan
if you want to

the crows lounging
in my yard
are glossy black
goddesses
and a river
fluttering like
a lazy man's sleeve
is also a part
of our world

the world
is so stared at
and its relations
and patterns
and your place
in the pattern
tall and happy
or crabby and fierce
you're an *occupation*
to your friends
who squeeze around you
as if you were
a crowded street
gathering together
the highest
and lowest restaurants

simple how a solid hug
gets made from
an invisible emotion
and a kiss on the cheek
is pure
yet important
as church bells
which are a summons
or a reminder
of the big stuff
and I'd ring them

for you now
if it weren't so corny
or possibly illegal
and the sound
would place
something human
in the Illinois air
which is so cold
and wide
it speaks of destiny

Responsibility and Rank

yours is for the flowers
in the Jewish hi-rises
at Oprah's house
for when the executive bankers die
and you're 50 now
still set on WXRT
and on the best imitations
"gimme fitty cent"
you ride your bike when it's 10
your phone comes and goes
like you do
but then again it doesn't leave the same echo
the golden liveliness that stays on
and I still see how you resemble
Dürer's self-portrait
the golden hair so insistent
it should be in a documentary on hair
and you too are a documentary called
"This is How to Walk Clear Across Town
Passing Only the Stuff I Like"
and here you are again
been to Paris and back just like documentation
and now you carry a new seal
happiness restored
because you've been blown on by French air

friend under dust and shining up again
I remember all about you
and return you
like a favorite doll
to the center spot

Sestina Salutations to Rodrigo Toscano

It is hot Rodrigo.
I think of brick
the sun capturing it like a hero.
I think of *oily*
the negative version.
Let's go out for lunch.

My favorite meal is lunch.
I'll make you, Rodrigo,
my companion, platonic version.
We'll eat at a chic place called Brick
where the food's not too oily
where the waitstaff have bodies like heroes.

It must be satisfying to be a humble hero
the kind without a Recognition Lunch
the librarian who crawls out of the ground oily
holding a small boy named Rodrigo
who fell through a pile of bricks
during playtime's deadliest version.

On Tutilla Island a version
of cricket is played. The hero
is the guy built not like a furnace brick
but like something more earthy, more like lunch.
He can bowl like this one Rodrigo
can dance. For spin he gets the ball oily.

I love when a fabric seems oily,
like silk can in some versions.
A designer named Christian Rodrigo
has a new line called Hero.
If I bought one thing I couldn't eat lunch
not even the mittens the color of brick.

If you were raised around Chicago brick
you'd understand it's a better atmosphere than the oily

fast-food for lunch
no-ethnic-types suburban version
of life spun around sports heroes
of life without the occasional Rodrigo.

Chicago's a city of brick, a version
of architecture not oily but heroic
a good place for lunch with Rodrigo.

King Kong Watches Over Me

Famous Shadows High and Low

Cole Porter

The famous shadow
of Cole Porter drinking milk
is a moon
his hat the flaming tip of the Chrysler Building
his shoes the iced lobby in the House of Concoctions

Batwoman

The famous shadow
of Batwoman on a slide
is a lollypop if you have the nerve
her bat hat like a hangman's getup
her dagger boots relentless as a spanking

Cult of Clarity

cabana necktie
orange death juice
on a silver salver
           this shows the death of a gangster

the double feature
doesn't make sound anymore
the film itself doesn't
           this shows isolation

a letter
in a red letter box
in the town that mail orders bras
           this shows isolation, the death of shopping

temporarily the two
of them were Serbian
then they were just crazy
           this shows how home became a ghetto

they have a fear
of cutting, stabbing
arms sliced off by steel
           this shows, like linked swans in an oven,
           their common bond

resting is when
the mind is dead
           this shows the unevenness of the body

the artist Marcos Raya
who made *Night Nurse*
lives close by
              this shows how awful it is to make "friends"

the sun
comes back
when it wants to
              this illustrates control

Frankenstein

Frankenstein naps on a golden bed
covered by a floral quilt
handstitched as he is handstitched

He dreams of making a gigantic sandwich
the tense moment of triumph coming when finally
he gets both hands to work at once

He dreams of picnicking in a glistening meadow
recently cleaned by a biology class
dreams of riding there on top a glistening Harley

He sees himself this way or else
prone in black leather
glamorously handcuffed inside his electric dungeon

Tomorrow he'll rise arms first from his golden bed
trying to piece together the images of his dreams
into an incontestable memory

When he stumbles toward you
will you slowly teach him your name
or will you quickly distribute fire?

Autographed Heart Forest

Dawn comes wild with swans swirling in a pool of thunder

Until the indoors offer something more arresting
you'll stay until manners distill
to a new conclusion

and strength itself changes meaning
here
no one who gives a heart gives a strong one

A peculiar heart
inside its irretrievable rib cage
is what I offer you

Look!
here comes my heart now
trundling along on the back of an old grizzly

And look!
the misty air
is crooning with thunder

from the great barbershop quartet in the sky
and at you
the Finger of Joy points accusingly

Porno Stars with Tuberculosis

At the Hotel Naked Lady
the sink is pink
and right next to the bed
covered by the smell of TV reruns

And instead of the Bible
there's a joke about walking across Russia
but it's in one of those Russian boxes
that's as difficult to open
as the cartoon egg of a solid-gold penguin

Flowers sit in a vase
and the floor is an ugly Victorian carpet
that pretends it is beautiful

It's best to read in a room like this
so your body does nothing at all
while your brain goes straight to the basement
its sweaty arms loaded down like a depressed stevedore
even though the sun is coming up

Movie Nun

If I were a nun in a movie
I'd want to be the one
eating cottage cheese intellectually
the one with keys to the pool

"Coins *never* rot," would be my motto
and I'd leave Greek weddings
carrying a plateful of feedback

For a fund-raiser
I'd write a wartime screenplay
where monks eat diamond biscuits
they later "deliver" to the French Resistance

If asked to direct
I'd show how a complicated nun
holding a simple wooden fork
prepares you to accept that starvation
in a fever jungle
hides within a lengthy and watery hymn

In the corner of despair
I raise my fist

The sun is rotten
the way it *illuminates* the convent kitchen
starving nuns of the joys of shadows
improvements eliminated leaving every fang

King Kong Watches Over Me

King Kong watches over me
kindly
benevolently
he bends his moist face towards mine
rocks his slick head quizzically
picks me up

His great hand closes me in
like a clam shell
but it's damp softness I feel
not a clam shell
the feel of an old soft dollar
rolled in old soft leather

King Kong watches over me
and I stare into his eyes
bloodshot and watery
two round brown pools
like the floor of silos

What is it he's trying to say
as I squirm and kick
like a female tadpole in his hand
he flips me over and looks at me backwards

King Kong watches over me
when he sets me down
ever so gently
onto a wet pile of hay
he watches me run to the farmhouse
close myself in
as I pull the shades
he bends to look in
babbling something in gorilla
which echoes across the farm

King Kong watches over me
over my house as I sleep
a dark organic monster
sliding through the moonlit cornfields
the slippery embodiment of exotic desire

Requirements for an Addiction to Movies

though layering macaroni and cheese
the woman is thinking of Hitchcock's layered motifs

friendship and betrayal
the grotesque and the ordinary

horror blended
with humor

for laughs
she dies her water Purple Nightshade

and drinks it like a movie star
in black silk pajamas

she attracts birds to her garden
with a giant projection of a black and white bread crumb

at night if the moon isn't there
she makes one from a round Albanian prop that reads

Gone to America
on vacation she visits theaters

The Silver Eye
The Dollar Shadow

at dawn she soaks in the image of a bubble bath
like an exhausted but beautiful murderess

she uses just one emblematic capful
of sharp-focus concentration

Oaf

he eats hillbilly tiger
and washes his red hair
with gasoline
he has promised to make a movie
to drive an Electra 225 onto a stage
and spit on it
to make a movie of this
to call it *Combat*

he has a taste for bone
and washes his grandmother
with rubbing alcohol
he has promised to take her to a movie
in her old Electra
promised her she could spit out the window

he drinks red oil
and fantasizes washing a mountaineer
with snowmelt
he was promised a movie of this
by a liar friend
he'd now like to spit on

he chews an orange blueprint of Tony Curtis
just exactly like a spy without a hat
or Nazi Beer to wash it down with
he has promised to keep the secret
so he only spits out the nonessentials
        the shoes
        the tip of the nose

he drinks from the pink water's edge and
as he promised himself
he laps it up like a tiger crouched at a watering hole
during an electric storm
when lightning spits blue strikes across the sky
        really

the sky is gray as a limb

what he doesn't know about sky, in general
    buckets
    London
    choreographing a face
    amusing a born Realist
    stomaching an aspirin
    the presence of Albuquerque
    sex laws
    jail agenda
    harpoons, in dreams
    limp heavyweights
    stone dead snakes and
    basements
could fill the Sacred Leg
and its nonelectrified cathedral

he eats crackers
on the steps of the cathedral
and fingerbowls in holy water
it's water dusty with promise
and he moves toward more of it
like an Electra 225 crushing a patch of jasmine
    the flower of promise
    the transport of joy

Permission Gardens

Quicksand death is the ultimate vanity
especially if it happens when the purple sun sinks
behind a frozen mountain

the last thing then
is an unaccomplished handshake
and the biggest deal falls through

sucked into a small inviting pool, calm as
a steady stream of uncovered corruption
ocher redesigned as a garden shadow

and surrounding it the vapor of a dozen kisses to each palm
and in silhouette an unruly clematis choking a purple urn
nervous energy drained into stagnant nobility

A slender streak of midnight
tucked behind the ear, however
becomes a temporal plume

for those who prolong sensation
when it's quiet and "anything is possible" seems probable
Raise a hand — ask for

open-mouthed admiration
mansions
vinegars

ask for the arrogant eyebrow
thigh-high confidence
the tongue relinquishing

Beauty and time
enter with zeal and decay and absorb the garden anyway
like old cleaning women with mops and carte blanche

Ask that time be perched
raise a finger to it
but not too closely

enigma should balance desire
so some euphoria remains always about to arrive
like rain in a drought year where

only a row of okra
grows in the muscular heat
a brawny blueprint for the abduction of sunlight

let desire bring a threshold to images
like fungi blindfolding the foot of a tree
to say where unseen things have been

My 7.5 Centimeter Delights

A privacy technician
closes the curtain
on the academic excitement
of fossils yet to be studied

For the paleontologist
in a basket-weave hat
the length of an egg
is its most interesting aspect

The scientific or aesthetic value of the
rotting effigy dress with tortoiseshell piping
depends on which light switch I throw:
what I like are mechanics that protect

A tremendous skull the size of a fingernail
something spectacular that can't quite decompose
found below the shadow of a decaying church,
the optical properties of this kind of social gathering

Zombie Jet

like the roofs of buildings
what's inside you
is beautiful and hard to reach
without the proper tools
the proper ukulele
the one Marilyn played
in *Some Like It Hot*
the one we all are sure
we too could play

and on Ukulele Mountain
many devotees
are presumably still doing so
waiting for jets to pass
to get a Shoestring Tempo

but the white dog in the window
across the street
hears this same jet and looks up
as if it could be a magnificent butterfly
or some other food
that's 10% treat
90% surprise

51% of today was walking
and 49% was lying down
exactly like a zombie
who must feed then rest
exactly like a pilgrimage
of zombies who must feed on a whole town
then rest in the field the town becomes
exactly like wandering hordes of zombies
who erase the rest of the world from
the light of day
but who cannot themselves
be erased

tonight there will be a quarter moon
a 10% promise and a 65% descent
into the section of the globe
that spins most magnificently

a night with a spiral staircase
echoing disintegrated chatter which
if you listen very hard
means squat
but if you listen loosely
is a cannonball of language
streaking across the sky like a zombie jet

Satan

In his red johnny one-suit
Satan moves out of the cool creaking sunlight
into the warm glow of the DeKalb Forge Company.

There, he's known as George
as a stud
a classic car collector

who carries a Cancerian love talisman
as a charm, who dates the beauties.
They all fall for him

for his sexy red wardrobe, his red Speedos
topped with a blazing red Bulls shirt.
He's a stud at the forge from 7 to 3

no furnace is too hot to work.
Like Hercules, he loves to bend steel,
and at night he bends the backs of his beauties

like big rubber dolls over his muscular arm
and asks them to go for a ride
in his old red Chevy.

They travel the road with him
unknowingly doomed, stopping at powder blue drive-ins
entranced by his chiseled features

and the way his legs never tire of putting
the pedal to the metal.
Satan likes the adulation of women

likes their cherry lip gloss
the way their hair can smell of apples.
They drive into the night

"Duke of Earl" on the radio
moonlit cornfields on either side, mega-agricultural
sentinels of the gateway to hell.

Little Lake Egypt

ecclesiastical and meandering the silver train
stops then steams
he places a hand on a silver arch

and leaves in a taxi
careful not to mess up his hair
knotting together glamorous lingo and holy bread

he grabs his luggage like a medical examiner
and cuts a grand path across the sand dune
as if he has the authority to permit

charm
to fall from pictures
because an arrow steaming in the lake

seems economic and moral
like a tattoo of a rock collection
he shoots an arrow into Little Lake Egypt

and sets his sexual morality onto comfortable sand
telling it to rest now
calling it Gardenia

then, fixated on the steaming arrow
he fantasizes about the woman with a bird's pulse
until he recalls he was stunned by the size of her couch

he abandons his luggage and hands a sea gull
the holy bread because it was kissed by a priest
whose breath is also a local punch line

tonight in the village
he will play poker with the Mexicans
who won't understand the last thing he'll say

Marie Antoinette Ocean

wearing heavy chunks of silver
and carrying a basket
they venture to Marie Antoinette Ocean

her eyes came here first by letter
when she wrote for reservations
requesting an ocean view

she requested vision in advance
as if light and its subsequent projection onto cells
that send a nerve impulse

could all be contained and marked
in elegant gilt script
RESERVED

his eyes were wrecked, hidden behind red lenses
which made him look decidedly tense
as if his demeanor were of the finest Swiss craftsmanship

his headache was gone as soon as they lowered themselves onto the
sand, taking pains to treat their lower backs with
the same care owners of rare foreign cars use in parking

they wore heavy gowns underneath their heavy chunks of silver and
they ate butter with tiny forks and dug out little bits of pomegranate
and shared these with one another

tide turning always made them want to read of discoveries
so she extracted a letter from the basket and made him see
cornfields fertilized by diamonds as seen by their correspondent

For LeFanu in October

green to the door
and a vampire who curtsies

take the blood away
and a musical instrument appears in her arms
a languorous musical instrument skinned in Spanish moss

the look she gives is a sequel to silence

look at her dress   clear as vodka

look at the room   brown as a burden

finally
it's raining so right cold-rocky cheerfulness
falls down the stairs
and the warmth of the other arises

Breakfast Sea

each day starts with a threat
desires evaporate in light
like a breath orchid weighed down by a decal

when the sun rises
the tendency is to curve toward courageousness
and to feed it little dishes of fear

so with a silver spoon
its handle shaped like the wing of a castle
we moisten our throats with the fog of self-absorption

coaxing persistence into our systems
assigning inadequacies a place
swabbing their own trap doors

at breakfast
before our faces float into position and focus
the fishy fear of ugliness complicates the pancakes

which sets off the fear of isolation
seen through a telescope as a black gown juggling cobras
in a sailor's wooden cafe

loss we simply toss overboard
for the braver sharks to digest
and in a short time noon heats up Monkey Island

a good place to concentrate on
especially when the orange monkeys seem
to be doing the rumba

Hedonism

versus grim reality?

anytime

take a long-haired dog

for example

devouring a cream cake

in a whirlpool

or a long-haired goat

in the Sudan

getting more sun

than any creature on Earth
wearing a bell

the sun is so close

if you think this way

you can practically own it

the answer

to give strangers therefore

is any answer

mist that is bland

as bad organ playing

can very easily

be concealing a vista

with so many

finger cymbals

even empty hands

will cramp

Accessories

1. REAL
Mundane Purse

The ugliest purse
is made of quilt-scraps
of cheap leather and contains no
scraps of paper on which is not written such words
as *Deep Freeze: giants fight for life in a world of ice.*

The mundane purse
contains Kleenex and keys
to an ugly car which drives its
owner to overlit places of business only.

2. FAKE
Hat from the Land of Movies

At the podium where it
will deliver awkward prizes to
an excessive number of children gracelessly
enduring the khaki army of childhood, the hat
from the land of movies is adjusted and then, like
a huge hovering electric monster bat, the word *Silence!*

3. ROMANTIC
Sacajawea's Gloves

A velvet curtain
the color of Shoshone Stew
opens to reveal Sacajawea's gloves,
which are in a lit display case. Like a

biker's knuckles, the knuckles of the gloves
have letters tattooed on them: B-I-R-D W-O-M-A-N.

But their leather is brown
and the fringe flays out not like
the spokes of a motorcycle but like the
fingers of a wild river whose countryside harbors
animals so tough all their names translate to *outlaw*.

Bigfoot

Bigfoot works in an Albuquerque egg factory
carrying the eggs from where the chickens lay them into
a frigid truck marked *Bob Walkoff's Egg Farm & Cheeses*

The little unfertilized eggs are as white as his huge body
which is covered in fur the color of Trinity sand
Bigfoot's passion is for people to love him

To name a pizza after him is not enough
He wants to be taken for a ride into No Man's Land
to share in the romance sunset here creates

On Saturday nights Bigfoot bathes in a sarcophagus
then pops out from behind birch trees
to see the sweaty neckers on Love Mesa

Their fuzzy dice on fur-lined mirrors
is an image erected to the passion of hope
but it cannot stop love and youth from fading

To catch a glimpse of Bigfoot
is thought to bring bad-witch luck to heavy petters
who often mistake him for an escaped mental patient

But Bigfoot only wants to hop in the back seat
and observe the workings of love
which can result in unwanted children

The children created on Bigfoot's nights on Love Mesa
often grow into spectacular elusive and lucky oddballs
who live quite successfully in remote sections of the globe

Cyclops Has One Gesture

It is the Evil Eye
It is moist and round

Like an ancient lighthouse
Cyclops is the center of attention

And so he is cocky
prancing around with a blind poodle in his pocket

Cyclops dangles a tiny red illusion
from his car keys

And at night
polishes the word *diabolical* with a green cloth

He is attracted
to things that shine

So works as the conductor
of the Vienna Boys Choir

Sadly, it's been years since he polished
the word *castrati*

But he takes solace each time the eyes
of the momentary sopranos focus on him

Alert and ready to obey
his ocular messages

Confessional Piano

Frédéric Chopin
wanted to be a girl
to be me in fact

you can tell
because of all
the high-Cs he used

and the peculiar thing
about this particular note
is that it makes my eardrum hum

but only the left one
and that's all
the spooky proof you need

Leonardo da Vinci Ocean

she lives in the north in a condominium
but she wishes she lived in the south
for the fiction and the swamps

she wishes daily with visions of an orchard
and travels annually to Leonardo da Vinci Ocean to see
the famous trees of the south growing in the sand

shaded, she sings straightforward love songs in Italian and
the guile her mother identified in her in childhood scuttles
away like a crab removed from the castle with a broom

her small muscular body is clothed only with a necklace
so her voice can escape also through her skin and
leaf shadows slip their pattern over her shoulders gallantly

at sunset, a blind-folded helicopter lowers her provisions
using the threads of a tapestry
a note inside gives directions for sleeping

she is to start with the normal process
first noting the constellations in one of many notebooks
then sleeping with a compelling smile on her face

at dawn visitors will arrive
clamoring for an audience
which she will grant or deny using the design of a bell